A Flower Fairy Alphabet

POEMS AND PICTURES BY

CICELY MARY BARKER

WITH LOVE
TO
M. W. T.

BLACKIE: LONDON AND GLASGOW

Blackie & Son Ltd., 5 Fitzhardinge Street, London, W.1
Bisnopbriggs, Glasgow

Printed in Great Britain by Smith and Ritchie Ltd., Edinburgh

CONTENTS

APPLE BLOSSOM

Up in the tree we see you, blossom-babies,
    All pink and white;
We think there must be fairies to protect you
    From frost and blight,
Until, some windy day, in drifts of petals,
    You take your flight.

You'll fly away! but if we wait with patience,
    Some day we'll find
Here, in your place, full-grown and ripe, the apples
    You left behind—
A goodly gift indeed, from blossom-babies
    To human-kind!

A

Apple Blossom

BUGLE

At the edge of the woodland
Where good fairies dwell,
Stands, on the look-out,
A brave sentinel.

At the call of his bugle
Out the elves run,
Ready for anything,
Danger, or fun,
Hunting, or warfare,
By moonshine or sun.

With bluebells and campions
The woodlands are gay
Where bronzy-leaved Bugle
Keeps watch night and day.

B

Bugle

COLUMBINE

Who shall the chosen fairy be
       For letter C?
There's Candytuft, and Cornflower blue,
Campanula and Crocus too,
Chrysanthemum so bold and fine,
And pretty dancing Columbine.

Yes, Columbine! The choice is she;
       And with her, see,
An elfin piper, piping sweet
A little tune for those light feet
That dance among the leaves and flowers
In *someone's* garden.
            (Is it ours?)

Columbine

DOUBLE DAISY

Dahlias and Delphiniums, you're too tall for
    me;
Isn't there a *little* flower I can choose for D

        In the smallest flower-bed
        Double Daisy lifts his head,
        With a smile to greet the sun,
        You, and me, and everyone.

        Crimson Daisy, now I see
        You're the little lad for me!

D

Double Daisy

EYEBRIGHT

Eyebright for letter E:
Where shall we look for him?
Bright eyes we'll need to see
Someone so small as he.
Where is the nook for him?

Look on the hillside bare,
Nibbled by bunnies;
Harebells and thyme are there,
All in the open air
Where the great sun is.

There in the turf is he,
(No sheltered nook for him!)
Eyebright for letter E,
Saying, " Please, this is me!"
That's where to look for him.

Eyebright

FUCHSIA

Fuchsia is a dancer
Dancing on her toes,
Clad in red and purple,
By a cottage wall;
Sometimes in a greenhouse,
In frilly white and rose,
Dressed in her best for the fairies'
evening ball!

(This is the little out-door Fuchsia)

F

Fuchsia

GORSE

" *When gorse is out of blossom,*"
   (Its prickles bare of gold)
" *Then kissing's out of fashion,*"
   Said country-folk of old.
Now Gorse is in its glory
   In May when skies are blue,
But when its time is over,
   Whatever shall we do?

O dreary would the world be,
   With everyone grown cold—
Forlorn as prickly bushes
   Without their fairy gold!
But this will never happen:
   At every time of year
You'll find one bit of blossom—
   A kiss from someone dear!

G

Gorse

HERB TWOPENCE

Have you pennies? I have many:
Each round leaf of mine's a penny,
Two and two along the stem—
Such a business, counting them!
(While I talk, and while you listen,
Notice how the green leaves glisten,
Also every flower-cup:
Don't I keep them polished up?)

Have you *one* name? I have many:
" Wandering Sailor ", " Creeping Jenny "
" Money-wort ", and of the rest
" Strings of Sovereigns " is the best,
(That's my yellow flowers, you see.)
" Meadow Runagates " is me,
And " Herb Twopence ". Tell me which
Show I stray, and show I'm rich?

(Hyacinth, Heliotrope, Honeysuckle, and Hollyhock, are
some more flowers beginning with H)

Herb Twopence

IRIS

I am Iris; I'm the daughter
Of the marshland and the water.
Looking down, I see the gleam
Of the clear and peaceful stream;
Water-lilies large and fair
With their leaves are floating there;
All the water-world I see,
And my own face smiles at me!

(This is the wild Iris)

(F

I

Iris

JASMINE

In heat of summer days
With sunshine all ablaze,
Here, here are cool green bowers,
Starry with Jasmine flowers;
Sweet-scented, like a dream
of Fairyland they seem.

And when the long hot day
At length has worn away,
And twilight deepens, till
The darkness comes—then, still,
The glimmering Jasmine white
Gives fragrance to the night.

J

Jasmine

KINGCUP

Golden King of marsh and swamp,
Reigning in your springtime pomp,
Hear the little elves you've found
Trespassing on royal ground:—

"Please, your Kingship, we were told
Of your shining cups of gold;
So we came here, just to see—
Not to rob your Majesty!"

Golden Kingcup, well I know
You will smile and let them go!
Yet let human folk beware
How they thieve and trespass there:

Kingcup-laden, they may lose
In the swamp their boots and shoes!

Kingcup

LILY-OF-THE-VALLEY

Gentle fairies, hush your singing:
Can you hear my white bells ringing,
Ringing as from far away?
Who can tell me what they say?

Little snowy bells out-springing
From the stem and softly ringing—
Tell they of a country where
Everything is good and fair?

Lovely, lovely things for L!
Lilac, Lavender as well;
And, more sweet than rhyming tells,
Lily-of-the-Valley's bells.

(Lily-of-the-Valley is sometimes called Ladders of Heaven)

Lily-of-the-Valley

MALLOW

I am Mallow; here sit I
Watching all the passers-by.
Though my leaves are torn and tattered
Dust-besprinkled, mud-bespattered,
See, my seeds are fairy cheeses,
Freshest, finest fairy cheeses!
These are what an elf will munch
For his supper or his lunch.
Fairy housewives, going down
To their busy market-town,
Hear me wheedling: " Lady, please,
Pretty lady, buy a cheese!"
And I never find it matters
That I'm nicknamed Rags-and-Tatters.
For they buy my fairy cheeses,
Freshest, finest, fairy cheeses!

Mallow

NASTURTIUM

Nasturtium the jolly,
        O ho, O ho!
He holds up his brolly
        Just so, just so!
(A shelter from showers,
    A shade from the sun;)
'Mid flame-coloured flowers
    He grins at the fun.
Up fences he scrambles,
        Sing hey, sing hey!
All summer he rambles
        So gay, so gay—
Till the night-frost strikes chilly,
    And Autumn leaves fall,
And he's gone, willy-nilly,
    Umbrella and all.

Nasturtium

ORCHIS

The families of orchids, they are the strange
    clan,
With spots and twists resembling a bee, a
    fly, or man;
And some are in the hot-house, and some
    in foreign lands,
But Early Purple Orchis in English pasture
    stands.

He loves the grassy hill-top, he breathes the
    April air;
He knows the baby rabbits, he knows the
    Easter hare,
The nesting of the skylarks, the bleat of
    lambkins too,
The cowslip, and the rainbow, the sunshine,
    and the dew.

O orchids of the hot-house, what miles away
    you are!
O flaming tropic orchids, how far, how very
    far!

Orchis

PANSY

Pansy and Petunia,
　Periwinkle, Pink—
How to choose the best of them,
Leaving out the rest of them,
　That is hard, I think.

Poppy with its pepper-pots,
　Polyanthus, Pea—
Though I wouldn't slight the rest,
Isn't Pansy *quite* the best,
　Quite the best for P?

Black and brown and velvety,
　Purple, yellow, red;
Loved by people big and small,
All who plant and dig at all
　In a garden bed.

P

Pansy

QUEEN OF THE MEADOW

Queen of the Meadow where small streams a
    flowing,
What is your kingdom and whom do you rule?
" Mine are the places where wet grass
        growing,
Mine are the people of marshland and poo

" Kingfisher-courtiers, swift-flashing, beau
        tiful,
Dragon-flies, minnows, are mine one and al
Little frog-servants who wait round m
        dutiful,
Hop on my errands and come when I cal

Gentle Queen Meadowsweet, served with su
    loyalty,
Have you no crown then, no jewels to wear?
" Nothing I need for a sign of my royal
Nothing at all but my own fluffy hair!"

Queen of the Meadow

RAGGED ROBIN

In wet marshy meadows
A tattered piper strays—
Ragged, ragged Robin;
On thin reeds he plays.

He asks for no payment;
He plays, for delight,
A tune for the fairies
To dance to, at night.

They nod and they whisper
And say, looking wise,
"A princeling is Robin,
For all his disguise!"

R

Ragged Robin

STRAWBERRY

A flower for S!
Is Sunflower he?
He's handsome, yes,
But what of me?--

In my party suit
Of red and white,
And a gift of fruit
For the feast tonight:

Strawberries small
And wild and sweet,
For the Queen and all
Of her Court to eat!

S

Strawberry

THRIFT

Now will we tell of splendid things:
Seagulls, that sail on fearless wings
Where great cliffs tower, grand and high
Against the blue, blue summer sky.
Where none but birds (and sprites) can go
Oh there the rosy sea-pinks grow,
(Sea-pinks, whose other name is Thrift);
They fill each crevice, chink, and rift
Where no one climbs; and at the top,
Too near the edge for sheep to crop,
Thick in the grass pink patches show.
The sea lies sparkling far below.
Oh lucky Thrift, to live so free
Between blue sky and bluer sea!

T

Thrift

VETCH

Poor little U
Has nothing to do!
He hasn't a flower: not one.
For U is Unlucky, I'm sorry to tell;
U stands for Unfortunate, Ugly as well;
No single sweet flowery name will it spell—
Is there nothing at all to be done?
" Don't fret, little neighbour," says kind
fairy V,
" You're welcome to share all my flowers
with me—
Come, play with them, laugh, and have fun.
I've Vetches in plenty for me and for you,
Verbena, Valerian, Violets too:
Don't cry then, because you have none."

(There are many kinds of Vetch; some are in the hay-fields,
but this is Tufted Vetch, which climbs in the hedges)

UV

Vetch

WALLFLOWER

Wallflower, Wallflower, up on the wall,
Who sowed your seed there?
                    " No one at all:
Long, long ago it was blown by the bree
To the crannies of walls where I live as
          please.

" Garden walls, castle walls, mossy and o
These are my dwellings; from these I b
          hold
The changes of years; yet, each spring th
          goes by,
Unchanged in my sweet-smelling velvet a
          I!"

W

Wallflower

YELLOW DEADNETTLE

You saucy X! You love to vex
Your next-door neighbour Y:
And just because no flower is yours,
You tease him on the sly.
Straight, yellow, tall—of Nettles all,
The handsomest is his;
He thinks no ill, and wonders still
What all your mischief is.
Yet have a care! Bad imp, beware
His upraised hand and arm:
Though stingless, he comes leaping—see
To save his flower from harm.

XY

Yellow Deadnettle

ZINNIA

Z for Zinnias, pink or red;
See them in the flower-bed,
Copper, orange, all aglow,
Making such a stately show.

I, their fairy, say Good-bye,
For the last of all am I.
Now the Alphabet is said
All the way from A to Z.

Zinnia

THE FLOWERS IN THIS BOOK

ENGLISH NAME	BOTANICAL NAME	NATURAL ORDER
Apple Blossom	*Pyrus Malus*	Rosaceæ
Bugle	*Ajuga Reptans*	Labiatæ
Columbine	*Aquilegia Vulgaris*	Ranunculaceæ
Double Daisy	*Bellis Perennis*	Compositæ
Eyebright	*Euphrasia Officinalis*	Scrophulariaceæ
Fuchsia	*Fuchsia*	Onagraceæ
Gorse (or Furze)	*Ulex Europæus*	Leguminosæ
Herb Twopence	*Lysimachia Nummularia*	Primulaceæ
Iris (wild)	*Iris Pseudacorus*	Iridaceæ
Jasmine	*Jasminum Officinale*	Oleaceæ
Kingcup (or Marsh Marigold)	*Caltha Palustris*	Ranunculaceæ
Lily-of-the-Valley	*Convallaria Majalis*	Liliaceæ
Mallow (common)	*Malva Sylvestris*	Malvaceæ
Nasturtium	*Tropæolum*	Geraniaceæ
Orchis (Early Purple)	*Orchis Mascula*	Orchidaceæ
Pansy	*Viola Tricolor*	Violaceæ
Queen of the Meadow (Meadow-Sweet)	*Spiræa Ulmaria*	Rosaceæ
Ragged Robin	*Lychnis Flos-Cuculi*	Caryophyllaceæ
Strawberry (wild)	*Fragaria Vesca*	Rosaceæ
Thrift	*Armeria Maritima*	Plumbaginaceæ
Vetch (Tufted)	*Vicia Cracca*	Leguminosæ
Wallflower	*Cheiranthus Cheiri*	Cruciferæ
Yellow Deadnettle (Archangel)	*Lamium Galeobdolon*	Labiatæ
Zinnia	*Zinnia*	Compositæ